Con

Who is St Gerard Majel...

1. St Gerard and the love of God in Jesus Christ   9

2. St Gerard and forgiveness   15

3. St Gerard and the sacrament of mercy   21

4. St Gerard and the Eucharist   27

5. St Gerard and the poor   33

6. St Gerard ~ the mothers' saint   39

7. St Gerard ~ a family saint   45

8. St Gerard and Our Lady   51

9. St Gerard and respect for others   57

10. St Gerard and the mystery of death   63

Novena prayer to St Gerard Majella   68

Who is St Gerard Majella?

St Gerard Majella

Who was this man, Gerard Majella, patron of mothers and babies, who has given his name to tens of thousands of boys and girls? It may come as a surprise to know that he was a young religious brother in 18th century Naples. Let me offer a brief outline of his short life.

Our saint was not the only child in the Majella family who was christened Gerard. A previous baby with that name had died in infancy. His parents soothed their sorrow somewhat by giving the name to their next son. They had no idea how that name and that child would become household treasures for millions throughout the world for centuries to come.

Gerard was born in April 1726 in a small village called Muro, about 60 miles from Naples. His father, Domenico, was a tailor. His mother, Benedetta, was a deeply committed Christian woman who loved God dearly and imparted that same love to her children.

Gerard was a happy child. He loved putting on

little plays, especially Passion plays. He would play the part of Jesus and get other children to actually strike and hurt him – that is, until his mother heard of it and put a stop to it. When he was 12, his father died and Gerard had to give up his schooling. For four years he was apprenticed to a local tailor, and was bullied and beaten by the foreman. Then the local bishop of Lacedonia was looking for a servant but no one would take the job because of the bishop's reputation for cruelty. Gerard volunteered, and stayed until the bishop died.

True to his reputation, the bishop treated Gerard cruelly every day for three years. Many would use such mistreatment as an excuse to quit the church. But not Gerard! He had a deep respect for the priesthood, but he knew the church was greater than any individual priest or bishop. In any case, he was glad to unite his sufferings with those of Jesus. And he prayed sincerely for his persecutor, just as Jesus prayed for his own tormentors. In 1745, at the age of 19, he returned to Muro and set up his own tailoring business.

But Gerard's soul was restless. He twice applied

to join the Capuchin Friars, once at the monastery where his mother's cousin Fr Bonaventure lived, but was turned down because of his delicate constitution. In 1749, when Gerard was 23, the newly founded Redemptorists gave a mission in Muro. Gerard was greatly impressed and applied to join as a lay brother. He so pestered the missioners that their leader, Fr Cafaro, advised his mother to lock him in his room when they were leaving town. However, Gerard knotted sheets together and escaped through the window. Twelve miles out the road he caught up with the missioners. He pleaded: "Take me on, give me a try, then send me away if I'm no good." Fr Cafaro gave in.

He sent Gerard to the community at Deliceto with a note for the superior, which read: "I'm sending you another Brother, who will be useless as far as work is concerned..." How wrong he was. Despite his frail physical condition, Gerard was an excellent worker. At different times he was gardener, sacristan, tailor, receptionist, cook, carpenter, and clerk of works for the new monastery in Caposele.

Gerard was professed as a Redemptorist on the

feast of the Holy Redeemer, 1752. He would die of tuberculosis in 1755; he was a professed Redemptorist for just over three years. What a wonderful gift God had given the new missionary order founded by St Alphonsus de Liguori! If we are to believe Gerard's family, his fellow Redemptorists, and the hundreds of witnesses who gave sworn evidence at his canonisation process, St Gerard was not only an incredibly holy young man, but one of the greatest wonder-workers in the history of the church.

While Gerard was still a novice, his spiritual director asked him to write down what he longed for more than anything else. He wrote: "To love God much; always to be united with God... to love everything for God's sake; to suffer much for God. My only business is to do the will of God." On his door, he pinned his life's motto: "Here is done the will of God".

Bro Gerard often went on parish missions with the priests. He could read souls, and confronted many a sinner who pretended to have made a good confession. There was a woman who had tormented several priests for months pretending that she was possessed by the devil. Bro Gerard saw through her. "Stop your antics," he said, "or to your shame I shall make known everything." There was no more nonsense from her. One of his Redemptorist colleagues remarked that "the success of a mission was guaranteed if Bro Gerard was with them".

More and more people sought out Bro Gerard for spiritual direction. Every spare moment he spent answering the letters of those who sought his advice. For someone they thought would be "useless as far as work was concerned", Gerard Majella's workload was amazing.

There's no way we could imitate St Gerard. He was uniquely gifted by God, for God's own reasons. But Gerard can point us in the right direction. His life can give us a sense of what the Kingdom of God should be like. God chose to manifest his power and compassion through St Gerard Majella. So, we have every reason to hope that Gerard will plead for us as he pleaded for the people of his day.

St Gerard, pray for us!

In 1893, Pope Leo XIII beatified Gerard Majella, and on December 11, 1904, Pope St Pius X canonised him as a saint. His feast day is October 16.

God so loved
the world that
he gave his one
and only son.

1

St Gerard and the love of God in Jesus Christ

In the first week of every new year, all the Redemptorists in Ireland gather to try and get our spiritual lives in order. A few years ago, we had a very memorable retreat. Many times the preacher shook the cobwebs off our old ways of thinking. One day he asked: "How many of you remember the Penny Catechism of your school days? What is the Catechism's answer to the question: 'Why did God make us?'?" Of course, we all knew the answer: 'God made us to know, love and serve him.'

Then he dropped his bombshell: "I would like to turn that answer upside down. It should be, 'God made us so that he might know, love and serve us.'" That made us sit up. Slowly the truth began to dawn on us. The first answer makes it look as if God needed servants or playthings to worship him and kowtow to him. Whereas the truth is God's only need was to give life and love to others.

Jesus said, "God so loved the world that he gave his one and only son" (John 3:16). This is the starting point of true religion. It's not about fear and judgement, or reward and punishment. It's about love – God's unconditional love for us and our response to that love. When the novice Gerard Majella was asked by his spiritual director to write down what he longed for more than anything else, he wrote: "To love God much... to do all things for the sake of God ... My only business is to do the will of God." Here he echoes the words of Our Blessed Lady: "Let it be done to me according to your will" (Luke 1:38).

There were two areas where St Gerard's love for God was especially evident: his total hatred of sin, and his passionate commitment to Christ crucified. How could mere creatures like us – he wondered – contemplate the life and death of Jesus and not be moved to the depth of our being!

One time, the bishop of Lacedonia sent a hardened sinner to the monastery at Iliceto to make a retreat. Gerard met the man on his way to Mass. "Where are you going?" he asked. "To Holy Communion," the retreatant replied. "To Holy Communion?" said Gerard in total disbelief, "and you with all those sins on your soul." Gerard quietly listed the man's sins and shocked him into finding a priest and making a good confession. The repentant sinner was back the following year, boasting that he had not lapsed back into sin. Again, Bro Gerard saw into the man's soul. "What in God's name are you at?" he asked. "Look on this crucifix. Who has made these wounds on Jesus Christ? And who but you has made the blood flow from the veins of the Saviour?" At that moment, according to the retreatant himself, blood began to trickle from Christ's wounds. Needless to say, the poor man was deeply shaken and this time his conversion was sincere and lasting.

Gerard's message for us today would be the same one he gave the Carmelite Nuns at Ripacandida: "When the Will of God is at stake, everything else takes second place." Everything!

Let us pray

Dear St Gerard, I kneel with you before the crucifix of Christ, my Lord and Saviour. I ponder his great love for me and for our ungrateful world. Dear Lord, forgive me for the times I doubted your love. Bind me now to yourself in bonds of love and gratitude. Never let me doubt your love again…

I kiss the wounds in your sacred hands
with sorrow deep and true:
May every touch of my hands today
be an act of love for you.

I kiss the wounds in your sacred feet
with sorrow deep and true:
May every step I take today
be an act of love for you.

I kiss the wounds in your sacred heart
with sorrow deep and true:
May every beat of my heart today
be an act of love for you.

I kiss the wounds in your sacred head
with sorrow deep and true:
May every thought in my mind today
be an act of love for you.

Forgive us our sins,
as we forgive those
who have sinned
against us.

2

St Gerard
and
forgiveness

It is all very fine saying that loving God means willing what God wills. How does that work out in practice? Let us begin with forgiveness. In the Sermon on the Mount Jesus said: "Why should God reward you if you love only the people who love you? Even the pagans do that." (Mt 5:46). In the Lord's prayer, Jesus taught us to say: "Forgive us our sins, as we forgive those who have sinned against us." (Mt 6:12).

When Gerard was 12, he was apprenticed to a tailor called Pannuto, who was very fond of him. But the foreman was a savage bully who reacted with rage to the piety of this young boy, and regularly beat him. On one occasion Gerard was knocked unconscious. Pannuto arrived on the scene as the boy was recovering and demanded an explanation. "I fell from the table," said Gerard. Sometimes Gerard would smile after a beating because he felt he was experiencing some of the suffering of Jesus Christ. That only infuriated the foreman more, and one day he struck Gerard with an iron bar. This 12-year-old child knelt at the foreman's feet and said sincerely, "I freely forgive you for the love of Jesus Christ..."

After completing his apprenticeship, Gerard entered the service of Bishop Albini. Working for him meant enduring a constant barrage of angry words, orders and counter-orders, biting comments, penalties and penances. Gerard took it all in his stride – glad to suffer with Jesus. When the bishop died after three years, no one shed a tear except Gerard, who said, "Sadly, I have lost my best friend, for his Lordship really wished me well." He could not bring himself to say an unforgiving word against his tormentor.

Forgiveness is easy to talk about. It is rarely easy to do. How can you forgive the person who raped you, or the person who abused your child? How can you forgive the drunk driver who killed one of your family, or the person whose lies destroyed your reputation? At the same time, lack of forgiveness can infect all our relationships and destroy our peace of mind. When we don't forgive, we remain trapped in our pain. Forgiveness frees us; it heals us. It is a gift to ourselves.

Put at its simplest, forgiveness is not a feeling; it is a decision to let go of the desire to get even with someone who has hurt you. With the prayers of St Gerard to plead for us, let us begin the process of forgiving whatever injustices or hurts we may have stored up in our hearts.

When Gordon Wilson's daughter Marie was killed in an IRA bomb blast on November 11, 1987, he said: "I have lost my daughter, and we shall miss her. But I bear no ill will. I bear no grudge... I shall pray for those people tonight and every night." That is true Christian forgiveness. We may not be able to say the words 'I forgive you' but we might say 'I bear you no ill will' and with Christ pray, "Father, forgive them, for they know not what they do."

Whatever the injustice we suffer, may we always follow the Christian path of forgiveness and let go of our desire to get even!

Let us pray

Heavenly Father, your Son emphasised that we should forgive one another. With the prayers and example of St Gerard to assist me, help me to see the hidden anger in my life and the painful memories that mar my peace of mind and inner tranquillity. Help me not to dwell on the wounds and the hurt that inhabit my heart like squatters; seeking to blame others and to assert my own innocence only leads me straight back to myself and away from you.

Lord, grant me the grace of a blanket forgiveness, even though I am not fully aware of how I have been damaged by the hurts of life. And where I fail myself, send down upon me your Spirit of healing and open my life fully to the blessings you have for me. As I pray that I might forgive others, forgive me, Lord, for I have so often disappointed you. O God, be merciful to me, a sinner!

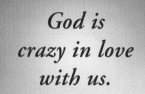

*God is
crazy in love
with us.*

··· 3 ···

St Gerard
and the
sacrament
of
mercy

Jesus, in his own person, reveals to us what God is like. He is like Jesus who would not condemn the woman taken in adultery but said simply, "sin no more". He is like the father in the parable who waited for his younger son to abandon his rebellious ways and return to his home where a welcome fit for a king awaited him.

Are there circumstances, though, when God's mercy reaches its limit? When a man confesses time and time again, "I might have had a drink too many," thus concealing his drunken rages and violence in the home, does God eventually go deaf to his plea for mercy? When a man or woman plays the role of the loving spouse and parent while secretly being involved in an extra-marital affair, does God eventually shut the door on their hypocrisy? Surely there's a limit to the sin that God can endure! No one can stand having their kindness abused day after day, year after year.

God can. God does. Jesus told his disciples there was more joy in heaven over one sinner who repented than over 99 righteous persons who needed no repentance (Luke 15:7). God is crazy in love with us. His mercy is limited by one thing only – our refusal to repent. That's all! Had Judas repented, he would have been forgiven. If a Nazi criminal truly repented, he would have been forgiven. It is stupid pride and arrogance to say that our sins are too great to be forgiven. Even if we arrived unrepentant at the threshold of eternity, God's mercy would try once more to melt our hearts with the fire of his love.

St Gerard used to get physically sick at the mere thought of sin which – as he saw it – renewed the suffering of Christ. He wished to take all the sins of the world onto his own shoulders and do penance for them. When he was near death, he began reciting Psalm 51, the Miserere, which contains verses like: "Against you, you alone have I sinned, what is evil in your sight I have done" and "wash me from my sin". In his last hours, he repeated these verses with great passion – sighing deeply, crying, and adding acts of contrition, as if he personally was the sinner. Poor Bro Andrew ran out of the room, terrified.

St Gerard is the patron of a good confession. As we saw in the first reflection, God gave Gerard an extraordinary gift of reading souls. Imagine if every priest had this gift! Would penitents come anywhere near them unless they were truly repentant? Would we try to hide our sins or play them down?

But the priest is only God's minister. Our true confessor is Jesus Christ and we cannot hide our sins from Jesus. Why should we – when we know that God cannot not love us, because God is love? Here's a question to ponder: does your Act of Contrition truly express your earnest sorrow and purpose of amendment? Or has it become an empty formula that you race through without much thought? Have you considered using a more heartfelt formula like "Lord, be merciful to me, a sinner!"? Or maybe look beyond Christ's minister to whom you are confessing and speak your sorrow, in your own words, to Christ himself who loves you and has died for you!

If you are burdened with sin, think of Jesus and the woman taken in adultery, think of the father of the prodigal son, and think too of St Gerard. Know that Jesus is only a breath away. Open your life to him and he will open his heart to you. Confess and ask forgiveness. He will not judge nor condemn you. All he'll say is, "go and sin no more!"

Let us pray

~ *An old Irish act of contrition* ~

God of mercy,
nothing is hidden from your
eyes.
I acknowledge in your sight all
the sins of my life
through the words of my lips,
through the thoughts of my heart,
through the grasping of my hands,
through every breaking of your holy laws.
I come to ask your forgiveness
in the sweet name of Jesus Christ,
lest I never asked it in sincerity before
and lest l do not live to ask it again.

4

St Gerard
and the
Eucharist

S t Gerard used to say: "The sick poor person is Jesus Christ visible; the Blessed Sacrament is Jesus Christ invisible." We turn our attention now to Jesus Christ invisible – Jesus in the Blessed Sacrament, in the Eucharist, in the banquet of life.

Gerard would have had no difficulty understanding the parable that ends with the wedding guest refusing to wear a wedding garment and being cast out (Matthew 22: 1-14). Everyone is invited to the Lord's table. However you must clothe yourself with good deeds and a life of faithful discipleship; as St Paul would say, you must put on Christ. For Gerard, one of the greatest sins was to approach Holy Communion in a state of serious sin – to come to the banquet without the wedding garment.

Gerard's relationship with Holy Communion began when Gerard was only five – long before he understood what the Eucharist was. About two miles from Gerard's home was the shrine of Capotignano. Many mornings the little lad wandered off there. In the church was a statue of Our Lady with her divine child. The child, we're told, would leave his mother's arms and play with Gerard. Before he left, the divine child gave Gerard a loaf of the purest white bread which he brought home. "Where on earth did you get the lovely bread?" his mother asked him. Matter-of-fact, he replied "Da un bellissimo ragazzo" – "from a most beautiful boy". The bread was obviously a symbol of the Eucharistic bread which he was, as yet, too young to understand.

Curiosity got the better of his sister Anna Elizabetta and she followed him and witnessed the episode for herself. Twenty years later, when Gerard was a Redemptorist Brother, he told her: "Now I know that the child who used to give me that bread was Jesus." His sister roguishly suggested he might like to return to see that child again and Gerard said: "Ah no! There's no need to. I find him everywhere now."

How true that was! Gerard found Jesus in the sick and the poor, those he called Jesus Christ visible. But above all, he found Jesus invisible in the Blessed Sacrament. Even when he was a teenager, his cousin, the local sacristan, lent Gerard the key of the cathedral so that he could come early in the morning and spend time absorbed in prayer.

As a Redemptorist, his greatest joy was that he lived under the same roof as Jesus. Receiving Holy Communion was heaven for him – literally. He was transported in ecstasy, his mind riveted on the mystery of God's redeeming love. This could last for a very long time. Only an order from his superior could bring him down to earth again. One day Gerard's biographer, the famous Fr Tannoia, was praying in the community chapel. Bro Gerard had to pass through the chapel to get to the other side of the house. As he did, he genuflected in front of the tabernacle. But he couldn't get up. He struggled and pleaded, "Please! Let me go! Let me go! I have work to do." And finally, says Tannoia, he succeeded in tearing himself away.

Habit and routine can suck the life-blood out of our religious practices. They can become dry, boring duties. Reading the lives of gifted people like St Gerard Majella can re-ignite the smouldering flame of devotion. The saints show us that it is truly Jesus, my Lord and Saviour, whom I receive in Holy Communion. Gerard inspires me – not to imitate him, but to stay faithful, even though at times I may feel faith-less.

Let us pray

Dear Lord Jesus, how I long to have a faith like Gerard's! I believe that you are truly present in the Sacrament and I wish to adore and love you. But so often my faith leaves a lot to be desired. I do not always honestly seek forgiveness for my faults and failings. I am a passive, distracted observer of the priest at the Offertory of the Mass when I could offer to the Lord all that I am and all that I have. I may even be totally distracted when the priest summons your real presence into the bread and wine. At that moment – I know – Mary and the hordes of angels and saints are transfixed in adoration at the miracle that is taking place before our eyes. Lord, through the prayers of St Gerard, increase my faith! And Lord, when I come to receive you, let it not be a dull, routine act, but each time let me receive you with love and tenderness, and surrender to you my heart and my life. St Gerard, pray for me!

*Help me
to help
them.*

5

St Gerard
and the
poor

S t Paul wrote: "Those whom the world thinks common and contemptible are the ones God has chosen – those who are nothing at all to show up those who are everything." (1 Cor: 1:26f). The first Christians were simple and humble folk, many of them slaves.

In the Roman Empire there were 60 million slaves. In the eyes of the law a slave was a 'living tool', a thing rather than a person. His or her master could torture his slave; he could even kill the slave. Slaves could not marry. Even their children belonged to their master.

Christianity was transforming all this. It gave those who had no life, eternal life. It told people who were useless in the eyes of the world, that in the eyes of God they were worth the death of his only Son. Christianity was, and still is, the most uplifting thing in the world. It is impossible to imagine a Christian saint not having a great love for the poor. St Gerard Majella was no exception.

When he started his own business he divided his income into three parts: one third for his mother, one third for the poor, and one third for Masses for the Holy Souls. There were times he gave so much to the poor that he went hungry himself for days. One day Gerard called to see his mother's cousin, the Capuchin, who noticed how poorly clad Gerard was and gave him an overcoat. Gerard had just left the monastery when he met a poor man shivering with the cold. Without a moment's hesitation Gerard gave him the overcoat. Of course, it earned him a fierce telling off from his relative.

As a Redemptorist, Brother Gerard had an opportunity to help the poor who came flocking to the monastery door. The winter of 1754-55 was particularly severe; more than 200 famished people came every morning and Bro Gerard's Rector, Fr Cajone, ordered Gerard to feed and clothe them as best he could. He was delighted with this task. As a tailor he could stitch together clothes from rags. In his eagerness to help, Gerard sometimes left his fellow Redemptorists without food. Several times, in answer to a whispered prayer from Gerard, God would miraculously fill the larder with enough food for the poor and the community. Witnesses swore they saw with their own eyes the loaves of bread multiply.

One of Gerard's favourite haunts was the Hospital for the Incurables in Naples. Gerard loved each patient as he loved Jesus himself, going from bed to bed, comforting and preparing the dying for their last journey. Those who were psychologically ill, in particular, took to Gerard. You could hear their excited voices through the corridors: "Caro Padre, dear Father, stay with us all the time. You say the loveliest things to us!"

When the poor are on our own doorstep, they don't always elicit enthusiastic concern. Like the priest and the Levite in the story of the Good Samaritan, we sometimes make up excuses to cross to the other side of the street.

Let us pray

Dear Lord, I know there were times when I had no sympathetic response to the plight of the poor. There were times when I said "Can't they go to the food kitchens" or "There's no excuse for dirt – soap and water don't cost much". St Gerard teaches me to see them as your children, sinners perhaps like me, but often without the opportunities that life has offered me. Help me to meet them, not as things but as persons like myself – no questions asked, no judgements made! Help me make time to listen to their stories. They were once happy children who played the games I played. They had families. They had hopes. Today they may be homeless – like the Son of Man they have nowhere to lay their heads. I cannot imagine what it's like for people who sleep rough if they get the winter flu; they have no warmth against the cold, no bed to sleep in all day, no one to bring them a hot drink! Yet, they are all your beloved children, Lord. As St Gerard used to say, they are Jesus Christ visible. Lord, open my eyes that I may see!

*St Gerard,
friend of mothers
and children,
pray for us.*

6

St Gerard
~ the mothers' saint

It is amazing how many people have the name Gerard or Geraldine or Majella. To this day, many miracles are attributed to his intercession. He is known for his protection of expectant mothers and is patron of mothers and babies. It is amazing that this frail, celibate young religious man should be chosen for such patronage.

Two miracles are singled out as the source of this reputation. One occurred during his own lifetime, the other after his death. In Senerchia, a woman was dying in childbirth. Her husband and family begged Gerard to pray for them, and both mother and baby survived. This miracle was carefully studied at Gerard's canonisation and was accepted as genuinely miraculous; the survival of mother and child could only be explained by a special intervention on the part of God, through the intercession of Gerard.

The other miracle occurred in a small place called Oliveto. Gerard called to say goodbye to his friends, the Pirofalo family. When leaving, he left his handkerchief on the chair behind him. One of the little girls found the handkerchief and ran after him with it. "Keep it," said Bro Gerard, "who knows, it may be useful to you some day." She was delighted to have her own special souvenir of the holy Brother. Years later, during her first childbirth, it was feared that both mother and baby would die. She had her treasured souvenir brought to her and no sooner had she held it than she began to get better. Her baby was born without further trouble. The woman's grandson inherited the handkerchief and he concluded his evidence at Gerard's canonisation process by saying: "My grandmother jealously preserved this miraculous handkerchief. Eventually it became my heritage; but now I have but a shred of it, as the rest has been cut up into small pieces for Gerard's clients." There were many more incidents besides.

Anyone with the mind of Christ must cherish the little children that God entrusts to them. Sadly this is not always the case. It is not the case when a grown man gives his 14-year-old daughter the full force of his clenched fist in her face. It is not the case when a drugged mother slaps her year-old baby to stop her crying. It is not the case when children live in an atmosphere of rows and violence every day.

I once watched a documentary about the work of the Irish lady, Adi Roche, for the Chernobyl children. I saw the exquisite love of Irish host parents for these poor mites, many of them cruelly disfigured and disabled; the gentle way they touched and hugged them. Right through the documentary I was crying and praying a heartfelt prayer of thanks for these wonderful people, and asking God to bless our womenfolk for their outstanding maternal gentleness.

Let us pray

Dear Lord, I pray for mothers who are expecting the gift of a baby. Through the prayers of St Gerard may they come to a safe confinement. I pray also for those who would love to start a family, that their prayers will be answered and that they may have the joy of bringing their baby to church to give thanks.

I pray for those who are contemplating sending God's gift back to God unopened – that is, those who are thinking of taking the road to abortion. Lord, help them to understand that a baby in the womb is as precious as a baby in the cot. If we spare our baby's life, it will not go unnoticed in heaven. However, Lord, if panic or fear or whatever has already made a troubled girl end her pregnancy, then let her know that you still love her and that you have a welcome for her. And I pray too for those homes where love is frugal or where violent language and violent acts are the order of the day.

St Gerard, you showed great loving kindness to children and delivered many from sickness and even from death – as Jesus did for the son of the widow of Nain; hear my prayers today and ask our loving Father to grant them for his Son's name's sake. Amen.

Family life is God's
way of teaching us to
become fully human.

7

St Gerard
~ a family saint

One day while Jesus was talking to a crowd of people, a woman cried out: "God bless the woman who gave birth to a man like you!" Reading Gerard's life we might be inclined to say the same about him. The truth was the other way round. Gerard did not become a saint by the touch of a magic wand. He was gifted by God because his parents had nurtured the soil of Gerard's soul in which the seed of God's love could take root and flourish.

Dominic Majella and Benedetta Galella, the parents of Gerard and his three sisters, created a deeply Christian home. They never had much of this world's comforts. What they had, though, was an abundance of faith and love, hard work and mutual support. Dominic worked hard to put food on the table and clothe his children, and to save what he could as wedding dowries for his daughters.

Where did Gerard learn his love for a kind and compassionate God except through the mirror of his own father! Where did he learn to pray except at the knees of his pious mother! When Gerard's dad died, the male figures that replaced his father were the opposite of what he had experienced in his own home. But Gerard had learned the lessons of Christian tolerance and forgiveness from his parents.

Family life is God's way of teaching us to become fully human. It's in the family we discover our identity in an atmosphere of love and acceptance. It is family who supports our decisions and encourages us when we are in the dumps. In a family our sharp angles are rounded off, our self-centredness restrained. Above all, it is in the family that we learn the importance of faith and prayer, by experiencing it in the daily life and decisions of our parents.

We are well aware of the mother's place in the home. But we sometimes forget the crucial role of the father as well. Their faithful love and mutual respect are the ideal foundation on which God's plan for the family is built. Without either one or the other, the task of nurturing a family becomes so much more difficult. We can only praise those single parents who have to face this challenge on their own and who, with courage and love, triumph against the odds, like St Gerard's mother Benedetta.

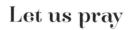

Let us pray

We remember our parents in prayer…

~ For a father ~
I thank you Lord for my father. Help me to appreciate the sincerity of his love for me and to be ever grateful for the sacrifices he and my mother made for me. Bless him with good health, with peace of mind and with long life.

St Gerard, you knew the warmth of a loving father. Help me thank God for my father and pray with me that all fathers may mirror the wisdom and love of our Heavenly Father and the selfless guardianship of St Joseph for the divine child. Amen

~ For a mother ~
I thank you Lord for my mother. I thank you for her unfailing love at every stage of my life. She was there to wipe away my tears when I was hurt or disappointed. When I did wrong she was there to put

me right. She is always there for me. Lord, be there always for her!

St Gerard, you are patron of mothers and children. Ask God to bless my mother and all mothers with every good gift, to give them health and peace, and the joy of being enfolded in the love of their children and grandchildren until they arrive safely and without fear at their eternal home in heaven. Amen.

~ Prayer of spouses for each other ~

Father in heaven, grant that my wife/husband and I may always love and cherish each other. May we bear with each other's weaknesses and grow from each other's strengths. And if we stumble through human weakness, help us to forgive each other as you forgive us. Grant us patience, kindness, cheerfulness and generosity to the poor.

(If there are young children: Help us to work together in harmony and shared responsibility in the rearing of our children.)

Father, I offer this prayer to you through Christ our Lord. Amen.

Mary,
our
mother.

8

St Gerard
and
Our Lady

As he matured, Gerard's relationship with Mary alternated between child and lover. When asked why he was so moved by pictures of Our Lady he said, "The Madonna has ravished my heart, and I have given it to her."

On one famous occasion – the third Sunday in July 1747 – the cathedral in Muro was packed for a celebration in honour of Our Lady's Immaculate Conception. Suddenly Gerard, aged 21, got up from his seat and elbowed his way to Our Lady's statue. His face was aflame, his eyes shone with an unusual light. All eyes were on him when he took a ring from his finger, placed it on one of Mary's fingers and said in an outburst of joy: "Now I am wedded to the Madonna!" It was a sort of mystical marriage, like those between many women contemplatives and Our Lord.

Mary is unique in human history. Out of the millions of girls on this earth, God chose one. French poet Henri Jordin put it like this: "When I sent my son on earth, he wasn't hard to please, about food or lodging or state in life or anything – except his mother. But about her he was exacting. He wanted his mother to be a masterpiece. And men are like him. Choosing a woman is always the great affair of their lives – which doesn't surprise me."

Mary had to be a masterpiece because she was "the means that God used to smuggle his Son into the world". All the honours and privileges that have been heaped on Mary spring from this fact – that she was the Mother of God made man and she said 'yes' when she could have said 'no'. But she is also our mother. She became our mother when she gave birth to Jesus, the Saviour. She was formally appointed to this role at the foot of the cross: "Woman, behold your son; son, behold your mother."

As every teenager knows, mothers can be infuriating at times. "What time will you be home? Where were you? Who were you with? What does he do? For goodness sake tidy yourself up! Clean your shoes! Hurry up, you'll be late for Mass! Set the table! Give over your arguing!" In many ways teenagers have a lot of experience and education. But one experience they haven't got is to be the mother of a teenager. Because, you see, mothers care. Add care to love and you have the makings of worries and anxieties.

We can often misrepresent Mary. We think of her as a kind of anaemic person: "Be it done to me according to thy word" may sound like a compliant, passive obedience to God by a woman with no will of her own. Such a notion is an injustice to God's taste and to Mary's character.

Mary could not have foreseen how her son's life would end – his arrest, his condemnation for blasphemy and subversion, his torture and his execution as a common criminal. But she had placed herself at God's disposal and as each new twist came in her son's life, she said 'yes' again and again.

Yes, mothers care. And the care Mary lavished on her son Jesus and on the early church, she gives to us now from heaven. Mothers don't come any better than the Mother of God, or as St Gerard called her in his childlike love: Mamma Maria.

Let us pray

~ *With St Alphonsus* ~
O Mary, conceived without sin, pray for us who have recourse to thee. Holy Mary, pray for us! Immaculate Heart of Mary, pray for us now and at the hour of our death. Sweet Heart of Mary, guide me to my salvation! Our Lady, Queen of Peace, pray for us!

~ *The Memorare* ~
Remember, O most gracious Virgin Mary, that never was it known that anyone who fled to thy protection, implored thy help or sought thy intercession, was left unaided. Inspired with this confidence, I fly unto thee, O Virgin of virgins my Mother; to thee do I come, before thee I stand, sinful and sorrowful; O Mother of the Word Incarnate, despise not my petitions, but in thy clemency hear and answer me. Amen.

Love of truth, justice and charity.

9

St Gerard
and
respect
for others

Nerea Caggiano came from a religious family. Now, the Caggiano and Cappucci families were good friends. So, when the Cappucci girls entered the Redemptoristines in Foggia, Nerea wanted to do likewise. Unfortunately, Nerea could not afford the dowry. So St Gerard, a friend to both families, begged the necessary money from his many friends, and off she went to the convent. She lasted three weeks.

Though she saw herself as a failure, she would not admit this openly. Instead, she hatched a plot to justify her action by pinning the blame on others. She began by criticising the nuns and their saintly superior, Blessed Maria Celeste Crostarosa. But nobody bought this. The problem was: if all these nuns were as bad as Nerea claimed, how come Gerard allowed her to enter there? So she turned on Gerard himself. In the spring of 1754 Gerard had stayed with the Cappuccis and that gave Nerea her chance. "Gerard's not as holy as people think," she hinted. She confided to Fr Benigno Bonaventura in confession: Bro Gerard had sexually abused Nicoletta Cappucci, she alleged. If that was so, said the priest, she should inform his religious superior at once. She was only too willing to do so.

Alphonsus sent Fr Villani to investigate the allegations. Villani interviewed Nerea and her confessor, who insisted that Nerea was an honest girl. He found no other evidence or allegation of any other misbehaviour on Gerard's part. Alphonsus sent for Gerard and read the accusing letter to him. Gerard never said a word. Here was a new and unexpected way for him to share in Christ's sufferings. While the matter was being investigated, Alphonsus forbade Gerard to have any contact with outsiders or to receive Holy Communion. Being confined to the monastery was not a difficult penance; it gave Gerard more time and opportunity for prayer. But to miss the Eucharist meant starvation for his soul.

Gerard's total trust in God was eventually rewarded. Some time later, St Alphonsus received a letter from Nerea Caggiano. She had been taken seriously ill and had confessed her calumny to Padre Bonaventura, who gave her as penance that she write the truth to Alphonsus. Her accusations had been a tissue of lies. The whole episode lasted about two months. When Alphonsus asked Gerard why he had not defended himself he simply quoted from the rule that Alphonsus himself had written, "When accused in the wrong, they will not defend themselves."

It is a serious fault to spread malicious gossip about people, even if the 'gossip' be true. But if the gossip is false and unfounded then it is the even graver sin of calumny or slander. It contributes to the condemnation of the innocent, the exoneration of the guilty, and the destruction of another's reputation which might never be repaired.

Far more sinister is the way people can use social media to bully and poke fun at one another, sometimes driving their sensitive victims to commit suicide. Maybe Mother Church should declare St Gerard patron of cyber-bullying – he would be exceptionally suited for the task.

Let us pray

Let our prayer begin with an examination of conscience:
Do I respect the reputation of others and avoid every

attitude and word likely to cause them unjust injury?

Rash judgements: Do I assume as true, without sufficient foundation, the moral fault of a neighbour?

Detraction: Without objectively valid reason, have I disclosed another's faults and failings to persons who did not know them?

Calumny/perjury: By lies have I harmed the reputation of others or, under oath, have I called on God to witness to a falsehood and so contribute to the condemnation of the innocent or the exoneration of the guilty?

Cyber-bullying: Have I been party to cyber-bullying in any form? Would I have the moral fibre to blow the whistle on perpetrators of this unspeakable crime?

Dear St Gerard, obtain for me, through the merits of Jesus' death, an unimpeachable love of truth, justice and charity. May God's Spirit remove from my soul any foolish desire to hurt others by innuendo or outright bullying. If I can help a victim of harassment, may I have the courage to do what is in my power to put a stop to it. I know I am weak, so pray for me that I may not fail. Amen

*In death
our lives will
be changed,
not ended.*

••• 10 •••

St Gerard
and the
mystery
of
death

Tell me, why are we Christians so afraid of death? After all, death is the crowning of all we believe in, the fulfilment of all we hope fo
I like reading accounts of the deaths of saints. You might ask why. Well, like Christ I want to say 'yes' to my death. I want it to be truly my final act of faith, no just a passive acquiescence to the inevitable. Reading about God's saints softens my natural fear and prepares me for a joyful return to our Father's house.

In June 1755 Gerard said to his doctor, "Doctor, don't you know that I shall die this year and die of consumption (TB)." He was already haemorrhaging badly but still he did the rounds of the archdiocese, requesting donations for the new monastery and church in Caposele. After six weeks of this gruelling work, Gerard collapsed. He returned to his monastery and was put to bed.

Gerard asked for three things to be brought to his room: a large crucifix showing the wounds of Jesus, a picture of Our Lady, and a paper with the motto on it: "The will of God is done here, as God wills it and as long as God wills it..." On September 6, he was at death's door. Now, for Gerard, the wish his superior was God's will for him. So, Gerard's spiritual director sent him a note ordering him to get better. And, unbelievably, he did. Gerard confided to a carpenter working in the house at the time: "I was to have died on the feast of the Nativity of the Madonna (September 8), but through obedience I am to live for 33 more days." After a week's recovery, Gerard fell seriously ill again. October 15 was the last day of his life. Late in the evening he forced himself to kneel and cried out, "There is the Madonna! Let us honour her!" Around midnight he died. He was 29 years old.

If Gerard had been a wonder-worker in life, in death the miracles multiplied beyond counting. Some years ago a lady I knew asked me to pray for her nephew Gerard and his wife Kathy Ann [names have been changed]. Their daughter, Amy, was just over a year old when Kathy Ann was diagnosed with cancer. If God was calling her home, they prayed that at least she might live until Christmas. Kathy Ann died shortly after Christmas. Her husband Gerard wrote this to his aunt:

"Nothing can fill the emptiness left by dear Kathy

Ann's death, but there are some invincible things I celebrate more dearly. I celebrate the new life which sparkles in little Amy's eyes. I celebrate the goodness of so many people who have reached out with genuine care. I celebrate my faith which is stronger and less selfish… I still have much to live through and work out. But I feel the strength and peace of a good God and a gentle Kathy Ann."

Whether it be St Gerard on October 16, 1755, or Kathy Ann and her family, they reinforce our faith that in death our lives will be changed, not ended, and the sadness of death will give way to the bright promise of immortality.

Let us pray

~ For a happy death ~
Dear St Gerard, pray that the good Lord will take away my fear of dying and grant me the grace of a peaceful passing from this life to the next, full of deep faith and trust like your own.

O Blessed Joseph, you took your last breath in the arms of Jesus and Mary. When the day of my passing arrives, be at my side with Jesus and Mary to guide me home. What I may not be able to say then, I say now: Jesus, Mary and Joseph, I give you my heart and my soul; Jesus, Mary and Joseph, assist me in my last agony; Jesus, Mary and Joseph, may I breathe out my soul in peace with you. Amen.

~ *When mourning a loved one* ~

Hold my hand, Lord. Walk with me through the loneliness and the valley of sorrow. Hold onto me when I am afraid to think about tomorrow. Let me lean on you, Lord, when I am too weary to go on. Hold my hand, Lord, through the night until I see the light of dawn.

Novena Prayer to
St Gerard Majella

Almighty God,
from his boyhood years
you blessed St Gerard with generosity of soul,
and led him to do your will in heroic ways.

By your grace he lived his brief life
in intense love for you
and for those in need.
Hear his prayers now for us
and for all poor souls in trouble.

Gerard, friend of sinners,
friend of the poor,
friend of mothers and children,
is our joy and consolation to come to your novena
to remember the goodness of your life,
your burning sense of God,
your tender love for Our Lord and his mother, Mary,
your kindness and care for everyone in need.

Pray for us now in our time of need.
Pray for us in our sickness.
Pray for us in our confusion and despair.
Pray for us in our struggle with life and its mysteries.
Remember especially those who long for children
and mothers about to give birth.
Remember those who have wandered from the
practice of the faith
and need the grace of reconciliation.
Remember all of us poor sinners in our particular
needs (pause).
Amen.

S·GERARDVS
MAJELLA

Further reading on St Gerard

St Gerard Majella:
Rediscovering a Saint

In 2014, Fr Brendan McConvery CSsR published an excellent new life of St Gerard Majella. The book is attractively illustrated by Fr David McNamara CSsR. While Fr Brendan treads gently on the very many extraordinary events that popular tradition and earlier biographies have recorded, he highlights Gerard's deep spirituality, his extraordinary familiarity with God and the heavenly beings, his abhorrence of sin, his passionate love for the poor, his desire to share in the sufferings of Jesus, and so on – all the things that made Gerard a saint before he ever worked a single miracle. This book is not a substitute for Fr McConvery's biography; it is a sort of supplement for those who frequently invoke the saint's help and prayers – a vade mecum of meditations and prayers. I hope that with Fr McConvery's illustrated biography and my little prayer book, you may come to love St Gerard as we do, and learn from him to live fully our Christian calling.

Available from
Redemptorist Communications:
www.redcoms.org • sales@redcoms.org • 00353 (0)1 4922 488

Acknowledgements

When one is a priest/preacher for more than 50 years,
one accumulates many ideas and quotations from other
gifted writers. When I prepare a sermon or write a piece
I am acutely aware of my indebtedness to others.
I cannot always acknowledge my sources simply because
I cannot remember them, but I do – always – offer a
prayer for them and theirs in gratitude. May the Lord
reward those whose superior wisdom and skills are placed
at the service of us lesser mortals!

George Wadding CSsR